Put Beginning Readers on the Right Track with
ALL ABOARD READING™

The All Aboard Reading series is especially designed for beginning readers. Written by noted authors and illustrated in full color, these are books that children really want to read—books to excite their imagination, expand their interests, make them laugh, and support their feelings. With fiction and nonfiction stories that are high interest and curriculum-related, All Aboard Reading books offer something for every young reader. And with four different reading levels, the All Aboard Reading series lets you choose which books are most appropriate for your children and their growing abilities.

Picture Readers
Picture Readers have super-simple texts, with many nouns appearing as rebus pictures. At the end of each book are 24 flash cards—on one side is a rebus picture; on the other side is the written-out word.

Station Stop 1
Station Stop 1 books are best for children who have just begun to read. Simple words and big type make these early reading experiences more comfortable. Picture clues help children to figure out the words on the page. Lots of repetition throughout the text helps children to predict the next word or phrase—an essential step in developing word recognition.

Station Stop 2
Station Stop 2 books are written specifically for children who are reading with help. Short sentences make it easier for early readers to understand what they are reading. Simple plots and simple dialogue help children with reading comprehension.

Station Stop 3
Station Stop 3 books are perfect for children who are reading alone. With longer text and harder words, these books appeal to children who have mastered basic reading skills. More complex stories captivate children who are ready for more challenging books.

More books by Ginger Clarke

All Aboard Science Reader: Bug Out! The World's Creepiest, Crawliest Critters

All Aboard Science Reader: Freak Out! Animals Beyond Your Wildest Imagination

All Aboard Science Reader: Gross Out! Animals That Do Disgusting Things

To Nancy & E.J., Heather & Philip, and Sarah
& Tony, for being fun, fabulous (not fake!)
friends—G.L.C.

To the young readers, I hope you enjoy
the pictures—P.M.

GROSSET & DUNLAP
Published by the Penguin Group
Penguin Group (USA) Inc., 375 Hudson Street, New York, New York 10014, U.S.A.
Penguin Group (Canada), 90 Eglinton Avenue East, Suite 700,
Toronto, Ontario, Canada M4P 2Y3 (a division of Pearson Penguin Canada Inc.)
Penguin Books Ltd, 80 Strand, London WC2R 0RL, England
Penguin Ireland, 25 St Stephen's Green, Dublin 2, Ireland
(a division of Penguin Books Ltd)
Penguin Group (Australia), 250 Camberwell Road, Camberwell, Victoria 3124, Australia
(a division of Pearson Australia Group Pty Ltd)
Penguin Books India Pvt Ltd, 11 Community Centre, Panchsheel Park,
New Delhi - 110 017, India
Penguin Group (NZ), 67 Apollo Drive, Mairangi Bay, Auckland 1311, New Zealand
(a division of Pearson New Zealand Ltd)
Penguin Books (South Africa) (Pty) Ltd, 24 Sturdee Avenue, Rosebank,
Johannesburg 2196, South Africa

Penguin Books Ltd, Registered Offices:
80 Strand, London WC2R 0RL, England

Text copyright © 2007 by Ginjer L. Clarke. Illustrations copyright © 2007 by Pete Mueller. All
rights reserved. Published by Grosset & Dunlap, a division of Penguin Young Readers Group,
345 Hudson Street, New York, New York 10014. ALL ABOARD SCIENCE READER and
GROSSET & DUNLAP are trademarks of Penguin Group (USA) Inc. Printed in the U.S.A.

Library of Congress Cataloging-in-Publication Data

Clarke, Ginjer L.
Fake out! : animals that play tricks / by Ginjer L. Clarke ; illustrated by Pete Mueller.
p. cm.
ISBN 978-0-448-44656-1 (pbk.)
1. Animal defenses—Juvenile literature. I. Mueller, Pete, ill. II. Title.
QL759.C53 2007
591.47—dc22
2007005072

10 9 8 7 6 5 4 3 2 1

FAKE OUT!

ANIMALS THAT PLAY TRICKS

By Ginjer L. Clarke
Illustrated by Pete Mueller

Grosset & Dunlap

Do you play hide-and-seek

with your friends?

Some animals play this game, too.

They also play dead or

pretend to be other animals.

People play games for fun,

but animals play to stay alive.

These tricks help them

hunt for prey or

hide from predators

who want to eat them.

Let's see how some really

weird creatures play fake out!

Chapter 1
Playing Games

The **cuttlefish** has big eyes

and a large head.

Its eight legs (or tentacles)

have suckers to help it grab onto prey.

The cuttlefish changes colors

to fool its prey or scare away predators.

Flash!

This cuttlefish puts on a freaky light show.

In less than one second,

waves of red and yellow

light up the cuttlefish's body.

The colors confuse a crab,

and it does not move.

The cuttlefish grabs the crab

with its tentacles and turns off its lights.

What a cool trick!

The **decorator crab** plays dress-up.

It covers itself in seaweed,

pieces of sponge, and moss.

This disguise makes the crab

look like the seafloor.

It helps the crab hide from

animals that want to eat it.

The crab changes its disguise

when it moves to a different place.

This decorator crab uses its claws,

or pincers (say: PIN-tzers),

to break off pieces of plants.

It sticks the seaweed onto

hooked hairs all over its body.

If the crab gets hungry,

it can eat its decorations!

The **porcupine fish** does not swim fast,

so it needs another trick

to avoid predators.

The porcupine fish is also called

a blowfish or balloon fish because

it can blow itself up like a balloon.

This porcupine fish looks like

a tasty treat to a shark.

The shark comes close.

The porcupine fish acts fast.

Poof!

The porcupine fish gulps water

and blows up into a spiky ball.

Now it is too big and pointy to eat!

The shark swims away.

He will have to find another meal.

This frog does something funny
to fool predators.
It looks like a normal frog
when it is sitting still.
Then a bird swoops in.

Hop!

The frog turns around quickly

and sticks its rear end in the air.

The frog puffs up and shows

the big false eyes on its bottom.

It is called the **false-eyed frog**.

False means "not real" or "fake."

These eyespots make the frog

look like a bigger animal.

The bird flies away.

What a great fake out!

This toad is also hiding something.

It blends into the weeds

as it rests in a pond.

Suddenly, a snake slithers by.

The toad flips over onto its back.

This toad is called a **fire-bellied toad**

because of its bright red-and-black belly.

It looks like the toad is playing dead.

But it is really warning the snake

that it tastes bad.

Most animals know that bright colors

mean a yucky taste.

If the snake tries to eat the toad,

the toad will ooze poison out of

small holes all over its body.

Most animals will never touch

this type of toad again after

they discover its terrible taste.

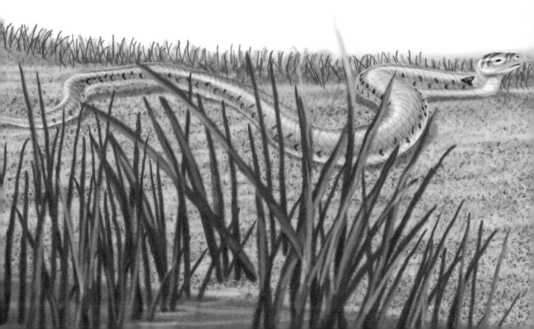

Chapter 2
Playing Pretend

To mimic means to pretend
to be like something else.
The **mimic octopus** can change
its shape, color, and texture.
It moves in different ways to pretend
to be a flounder, lionfish, crab,
or other sea creatures.

This mimic octopus is about to be
attacked by a group of damselfish.
The octopus quickly hides in a hole
on the bottom of the ocean.
It sticks two tentacles out of the hole
and waves them around.
The octopus is pretending to be
two banded sea snakes.
Banded sea snakes eat damselfish.
The damselfish swim away fast!

The **leafy sea dragon** is a fish
related to the sea horse.
The sea dragon pretends to be
a piece of seaweed or kelp.
Its leaflike fins help it
blend in with the kelp.
These fins are not used to swim.

This sea dragon stays very still
and waits for food to swim by.
It hardly moves at all except
to sway like a piece of kelp.
Tiny creatures called krill
do not see the sea dragon.
Slurp!
The sea dragon sucks up the
krill with its long snout.

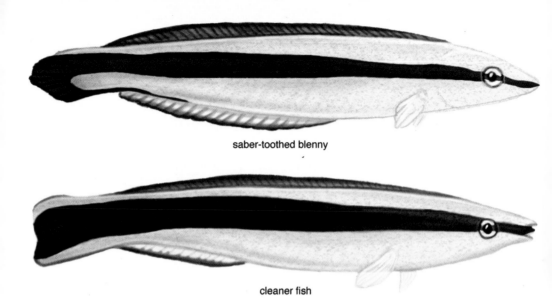

saber-toothed blenny

cleaner fish

The **saber-toothed blenny**

looks like a cleaner fish.

Cleaner fish eat bugs that live on

the bodies of other large fish.

When a cleaner fish sees a big fish,

it does a special zigzag dance

to let the other fish know

that it can clean it.

Because the saber-toothed blenny

looks like a cleaner fish,

it can play a nasty trick.

This blenny does the cleaner-fish dance.

A larger fish swims up to be cleaned.

But instead of cleaning the fish,

the blenny takes a bite of it

with its two big fangs.

Ouch!

This caterpillar will grow up
to be a hawk moth.
But for now it needs to keep from
being eaten by birds and lizards.
So the **hawk moth caterpillar**
pretends to be another animal.

This caterpillar sees a lizard coming close.

It turns around and wiggles its tail.

The caterpillar's rear end looks like

the head of a viper snake.

The large, black eyespots surprise

the lizard, and it backs off.

The lizard was fooled by a fake snake!

Can you tell which one

of these bugs is a real ant?

The one on the left is an ant.

The one on the right is a spider!

Some types of bugs pretend to be ants

so they will not get eaten.

Some ants can bite and sting,

so most insect eaters avoid them.

Other bugs blend in with the ants

so they can enter the ants' nest

and eat the ants.

This spider has an antlike body.

It is called an **ant-mimic spider**

because it acts like an ant.

But the spider has eight legs,

and ants have only six legs.

The spider waves its two front legs

over its head to look like ant feelers.

The ants think the spider is one of them.

Pow!

The spider pounces and eats the ants.

What a sneaky trick!

Chapter 3
Playing Dead

Many predators will not eat
animals that are already dead.
So some creatures pretend to die
when they are attacked
to keep from being eaten.

A red-tailed hawk swoops in and

tries to grab this **hognose snake**.

The snake hisses and puffs up its neck.

If this does not scare off the hawk,

the snake flops over and plays dead.

It hangs its tongue out of its open mouth.

Then it lets out a stinky liquid

from its rear end so it smells dead.

Phew!

When the hawk flies off,

the snake flips over and slithers away.

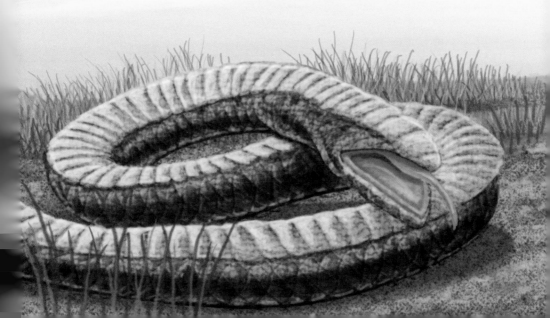

The **fainting goat** falls over
when it gets excited or scared.
We are not sure why the fainting goat
does this, but it might be playing dead
so other animals will leave it alone.

These fainting goats see a big dog
running toward them.

Some of them fall over.

It looks like they are fainting.

They fall because the muscles
in their legs get stiff.

When their muscles relax again,
they can stand back up easily.

This does not hurt the goats,
but it sure looks funny!

Big-eared bats eat insects.
They swoop around at night
scooping up bugs
and sleep during the day.
In the winter, there are no
insects for the bats to eat,
so the bats have to hibernate.

These big-eared bats hang together

in a group from a cave ceiling.

They are hibernating.

Animals that hibernate sleep

for the whole winter

to save up their energy.

Hibernating is like playing dead

because the animals do not eat or move.

The bats will sleep until springtime.

That's a loooong nap!

There are many kinds of plover birds.

Many of them are sneaky.

When a plover sees a predator,

it pretends to be hurt.

This trick confuses the predator,

so the plover can get away safely

and protect its young.

This **piping plover** sits on its nest.

A fox is lurking nearby.

It wants to eat the plover's eggs.

The plover hops up and acts hurt.

It pretends to have a broken wing

and leads the fox away from its nest.

The fox tries to catch the injured bird.

But once the plover brings the fox

far enough away, it flies off

and returns to its nest.

What good acting!

Is that a dead leaf

lying on the seabed?

No.

It is a leaf fish.

This fish acts like a dead leaf

so it can hide from its prey.

It even floats instead of swims

to look like a sinking leaf.

Some leaf fish can change colors

to match different leaves.

This **Caribbean leaf fish** rests quietly.

A small fish swims nearby.

The leaf fish wiggles its

see-through tail fin to get closer.

The little fish does not see

the leaf fish coming.

Slurp!

The leaf fish opens its big mouth

and sucks in the smaller fish.

Chapter 4
Playing Hide-and-Seek

Many chameleons can change
the color of their skin.
This is called camouflage
(say: KAH-mo-flazh).
Camouflage helps the chameleons
hide in the trees as they wait for prey.
Chameleons can also change color when
they are cold, hot, or excited.

This **panther chameleon** is
ready for a snack.
It spots a fly with its big eyes.
The fly does not see the
green-and-brown chameleon
hiding on a tree branch.
Zap!
The chameleon shoots out
its long, sticky tongue
and grabs the fly.

Do you see an animal
hiding in the snow?
It is an **arctic fox**.
This fox's thick coat keeps it
warm in the freezing cold winter.
Because the fox's coat is white,
it also provides camouflage.
The fox can hunt for birds
and hide from polar bears.

In the summer, the snow melts.

The arctic fox sheds its

thick, white winter fur

to stay cool and blend in.

Now the fox is mostly brown and gray.

Its fur will change back to white

when it gets cold again.

The **horned frog** sits still
on the forest floor.
It is hard to see because its
brown body and pointed head
look like a leaf.

This horned frog rarely moves,

except when prey passes by.

A scorpion scurries around.

It does not see the frog.

Suddenly, the horned frog hops up

and gulps down the scorpion.

After the frog finishes eating,

it sits still again and waits for more prey.

A larva is a wormlike baby insect.

The larva for the caddis fly,

or **caddis worm**,

builds a house around itself

to hide from predators.

There are many types of caddis worms.

They all live underwater.

Different types of worms use different

things to make their underwater houses.

These worms attach stones, shells, twigs,

and seaweed around their sticky bodies.

This keeps them safe from

fish that want to eat them.

The fish are faked out,

and they swim on by.

The **peacock flounder** is a flatfish.
Flatfish can match different
patterns on the ocean floor
to hide from predators.
The peacock flounder mimics
the look of pebbles and sand.
It can look almost invisible!
The peacock flounder is so good
at disguising itself that
it can even match a checkerboard.

This flounder hides on

the bottom of the ocean.

It is hard to see because

it matches the color of the sand.

Only its eyes stick up.

When a shrimp passes by,

the flounder pops up.

Chomp!

It munches the shrimp.

A **flower mantis** is a type of
praying mantis that lives on flowers.
It uses camouflage to hide
in the center of a flower.
Its legs and body look like
the petals of the flower.

Bzzzz!

A bumblebee zooms into

the center of a big white flower.

It lands for a drink of nectar.

Suddenly, the bee is snatched up!

A flower mantis was hiding

inside the flower.

The mantis munches its lunch.

Then it crawls back into

the middle of the flower

and waits quietly.

Sometimes the world around us
is not what it seems to be.
Many creatures use disguises
or play clever tricks.
Some are hiding to stay alive.
Others are just waiting
for a meal to wander by.